Sleeping Woman

Books by Herbert Scott

Disguises
Durations
Groceries

Sleeping Woman

Herbert Scott

Carnegie Mellon University Press
Pittsburgh 2005

Acknowledgments

The author is grateful to the editors of the following publications in which certain of these poems originally appeared:

Black Warrior Review, Caliban, CutBank, Hearse, The Kenyon Review, Michigan Quarterly Review, New England Review, Nimrod, Ploughshares, Poetry Northwest, Poetry Now, Shenandoah, Verse, The Virginia Quarterly Review

Contemporary Michigan Poetry, Wayne State University Press, Detroit, MI
How Much Earth, Roundhouse Press, Berkeley, CA
Looking for Your Name, Orchard Books, New York, NY
New Poems from the Third Coast, Wayne State University Press, Detroit, MI
Preposterous, Orchard Books, New York, NY

In the Palm of Space, Sutton Hoo Press, Winona, MN; fine press, limited edition

The author wishes to thank Rebecca Beech, Tricia Hennessy, Michele McLaughlin, and Arnie Johnston; also New Issues stalwarts David Dodd Lee, Margaret von Steinen, Marianne Swierenga, Lynnea Page, Derek Pollard, and Jonathan Pugh. Special thanks to Jerry Costanzo for asking to see this manuscript, and to Western Michigan University for a lifetime of generous and kind colleagues and students. A deep bow to friends, newfound and old, in Kalamazoo and Carbondale.

Design: Tricia Hennessy, Production: Paul Sizer
The Design Center, School of Art, Western Michigan University

Publication of this book is supported by a grant from the Pennsylvania Council on the Arts.

PENNSYLVANIA COUNCIL ON THE ARTS

Library of Congress Control Number: 2004100918
ISBN 0-88748-430-1 Pbk.

Printed and bound in the United States of America

10 9 8 7 6 5 4 3 2 1

Contents

I

II

III

IV

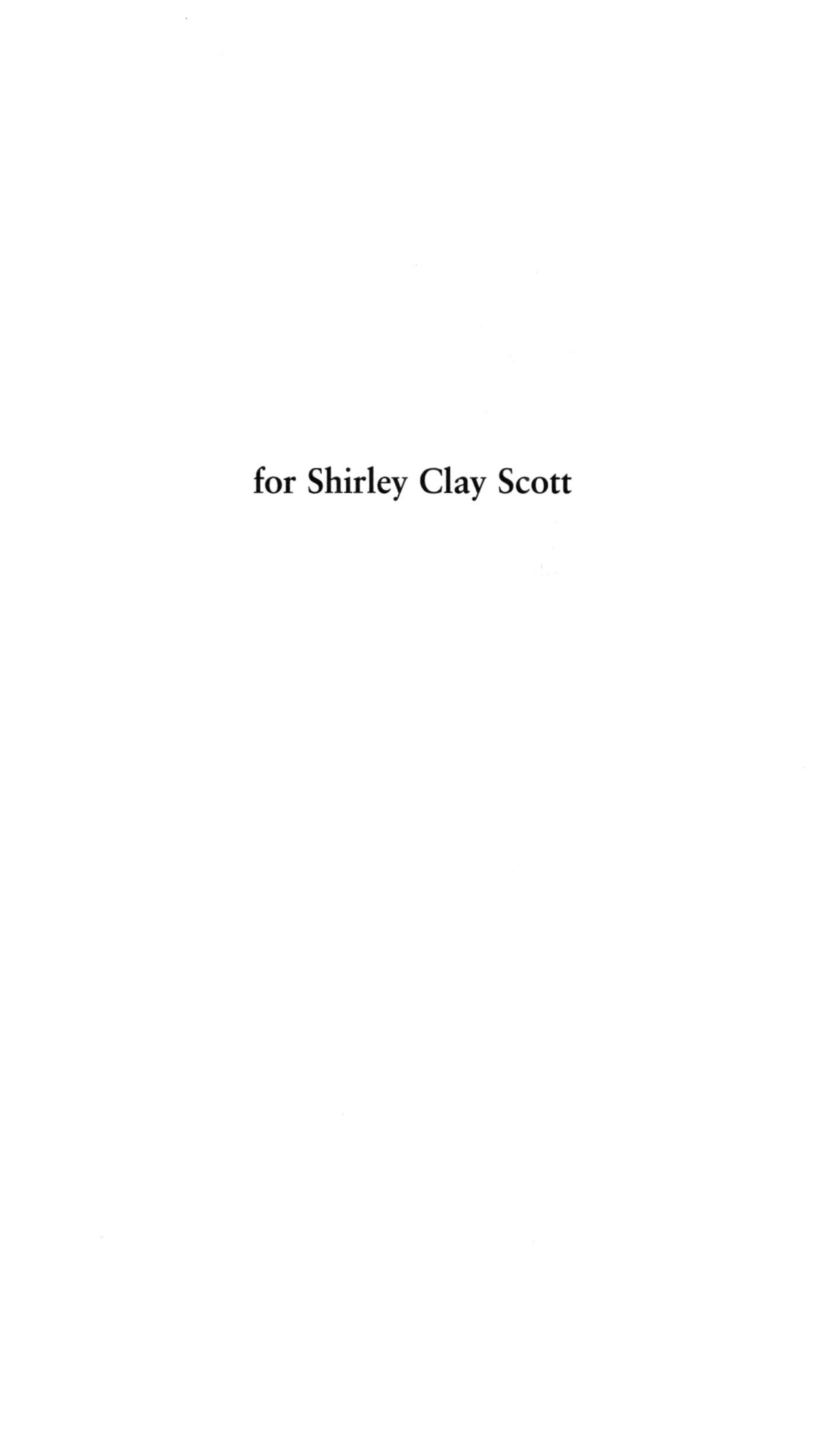

for Shirley Clay Scott

Invocation

Skin, and bone, and weed
flower in the flesh.
Do not go to sleep.

Love is a dust we keep,
silt of the body's dreaming.
Do not go to sleep.

If I were the speech of leaves
I'd let my body sing.
Do not go to sleep.

Words like willow branches
bend to the earth's reach.
Do not go to sleep.

Sleeping Woman

after the painting by Richard Diebenkorn

I'm walking east down Lovell in Kalamazoo
in the middle of the afternoon, and it's hot, July
something, and there's a man sleeping on the sidewalk—
the way you would in your bed—his body a kind of Z
in a fancy serif font, the curlicue of hands
beneath his head at the top, and the toes of each foot
curved to comfort the other, at the bottom. At first
I don't know if he's alive or dead, his skin
the color of burnt iron, a darkness alcohol finally brings.
I remember him from months before, a couple of blocks
west of here. He leaned against my car and wanted
to borrow money, a loan. He wanted a ride to South Haven
where he could get the money to pay me back.
His voice had that desperate familiarity that says:
You know me. You must want to care for me.
I think I gave him something, not much, and drove away.
I couldn't forget his face, murky with solitude,
like the hard red clay in Oklahoma where I grew up
that won't grow anything—everything lost to erosion
that brings such desolation you can't survive.
I thought he wouldn't survive more than a week or so,
but here he is, and when the cops arrive they know him,
call him Billy, and he's still alive, maybe
for the last time, and they pick him up.
I head east again, turn left into the cool museum
where I lose myself, sometimes, where I find you
sleeping where I've seen you before, paint streaming
around you like water, gathering in the shallows
of your dress. I am always surprised to see you.
I don't know. Are you flesh, or water? If I move
you will disappear in a startle of color.

The gallery is almost dark—those new-fangled spots
that keep the viewer anonymous—but your face turns
toward me from the crook of your doubled arms,
all about you an unencumbered sway, an intelligence
of light explicit as a summer evening. Deer quietly chewing.
I balance, in the shadows, between.

The Unforgiven

It is strange
how sometimes
no matter
if we live for years
a good and loving life
we are never forgiven
our smallest transgressions

those first wavering steps
in the wrong direction
never to be brought back

although we stand
in the unlit doorway
late into the darkness
calling down
the narrow
and otherwise
empty street.

Mime

That feeling of someone there
so she turns to peer over her shoulder
but the sidewalk clicks empty
and no one at the open window she passes.
Still, that unease, like the distress
of curtains settling, the failing lung of air
as she turns again, and, oh, there is
someone, someone familiar,
as if she has stepped aside
and sees herself as she might be.
It must be one of those street mimes,
one of those who gather a living
becoming what one cannot become,
becoming her walk, her grace
and particularity, her flesh
as it furls and dips, playing
to those who watch just out of reach,
with a smirk, with shoulders winking,
arms straight at the sides
but the hands tipped outward,
spilling the cooled tea;
so that as she turns
there is only that figure turning
in pirouette, its skirt wheeling
in the brilliant silk of motion, the face
already lost in the unaccountable distance.

In a Field of Sunlight

We will walk into the field
of goldenrod splintered
by the sun's foolishness.
We have been there before,
after a rain,
when the water streamed
like the grain of wood
around obliterations
of limb, and knots
of mourners recalling
other losses, other rains.

The mind as it chills
returns to sunlight
and the child's leaping stitch
across the field,
bobbing above weeds
and remorse, until we go
to meet her
where she progresses,
where she rises
into the arms' reach,
her gnatty hair gleaming.

Dream

Each rinse of morning light becalms the surf
that washes up loose kelp, dead fish, a sailor's cap,

or bobbers blown of glass encased in rope, loosed
from moorings near Japan, flotsam. Sleep takes whatever

comes, nurtures rubbish, weeds, the ways a dreamer spins
a halo of unlikely mettle around the body's archipelago.

Nude on a Kitchen Stool

Knee up, herself
apart from the air

her flesh dispenses
its own revolutions

intersecting moons.
Not a train on a siding

or a spoon banging
a tin pie plate

but a moon dividing
her body in porcelain blooms.

Late Fall, Rain

The rain is picking its switches,
beating the chrysanthemums
for their own good.

The eye can see only in muted lines,
disappearances. The sidewalks
are busy giving directions.

What have we to lose?
An old raccoon climbs
from the storm sewer,

bumbles a trail of piss
across the porch, the welcome
mat: a usual visitor. Enter:

someone's daughter foggy
in yellow warm-ups, jogging.
She is the last word autumn utters.

Bees

The bees found an entrance below
the eavestrough, a passage
where the stucco gaped an invitation
early last fall, too late,
I would think, to establish
winter store. Their business
kept me away from overflowing
leaves wedging drains,
so that autumn rains brewed
and rose and fell
into window wells two stories below.
And I with no courage or will
to force their fury
let them build and save
until winter closed the door,
then bought the poison to apply.
With ladder, spray, and caulk
I sealed them in their vault and thought:
this is the last of it. But in the nights
that followed, that turned to months,
in that dark house I listened
to their darkness, their blind assault
that seemed like sleet within the walls,
those starved, bony bees chalking
their maze, marking blind alleys
again and again, until I longed
for any way to wrench them loose,
set them free, stop their ticking.
When would they settle, give in,
begin to write their pleas
for forgiveness, their wills?
With what mute remonstrance
would they inhabit
that numb peace before drowning?

November

It is raining today, the slick
whale backs of sidewalks
surfacing along the block.
Look how the earth throws them
up, buckled, breaking. The fallen
leaves, raked into humps, flatten,
press down like hands.
If I were to reach my hand
into the rich, wet leaves
and lift them to my face, I would smell
the season's blood, animal, insect,
the evidence of earthly living.
Each thing has left its mark, its scent,
all the ravelled fragments of birth
and death fallen into place.
North of here, November glistens, a new
snow sticking to everything: branches
of trees, cats curled on porches, the
steaming backs of horses. Distance turning
rain to snow or snow to rain. Each
is pain and beauty, wet pavement glowing
in the pale November noon, or snow its own
illumination, each winding across time
and distance a dark path.

Neighbor

For years he has tilled his yard,
his wife and two children
the fruit of his labor, a dog
behind the chain-link fence.
We are cordial: Yes, we must get together.
We nod, his wife nods.
As I drive by
on my way to work he waves
like a friendly guard at the border.
Once I saw eighteen canoes stacked
in his yard. A scouting trip
up north, I think. Twice
he was operated on for cancer.
I know little else about him.
We are set apart like our two houses.
And today, seeing him in his yard
for the thousandth time, raking leaves,
red hunting jacket ablaze in the autumn light,
his dark-browed face bent to his task,
I felt a sudden snap,
as if something had closed
for the last time. It felt
involuntary as a swallow,
something that quick and ordinary,
and I knew an irretrievable distance.
I would never lie down beside him,
drunk with wine and silence.
I would never take his wife into my arms,
saying *sorry, sorry.*

Night Walking

The nose
of an oboe

a wedge of light
through an open door

darkness
pried apart

a kind
of breathing

voices
of houses

the street
a patient silence

and that long, thin
reed of music

something you
nod to, passing

fingers pigeoned
in front pockets

as though it were
your song.

And the Sleet Cometh Down

i

Her skull a white stone
flower set in a slender vase,
her face, the planes
of forehead and cheek, the apple
of her chin, unadorned by skin
or color. I would lay my hand
across the formal brow, feel
the cold, curved bone taking
my skin and flesh until nothing
remains but bone upon bone.
And the caves of her eyes,
if there are eyes,
cheeks, even without flesh, curved
and high, and the only color
a thick red wrist of hair
plaited down the back
of the skull, laid carelessly across
the front of her left shoulder.

ii

A tug on the river
makes a mosaic of ice
after the winter storm
warning us into our own
warm bodies, the prow plotting
the ice into new design,
a mortar of water sealing
the passage, as the final breath
hazes the glass where one finger
could pulse a new channel,
like a tug whose whistle

heard from this room
resounds between memory
and what is.

The Story of Bread

The peasants know bread,
how it breaks beneath their hands,

the long, thick nails that harden and sprout
like the splayed hooves of their horses.

In the fields they bend to lift stones,
heavy loaves their plows have turned.

Brown is the earthen smell, brown the faces
and hands of workers in the weather's oven.

Inside the small huts women sink into bowls
of quick dough, their brows marked

by strange signs. Children, sweet as muffins,
suckle at their nipples. Will these little loaves

of hunger never stop rising from their bellies?
At night they squeal from their cribs like air

while on the tables of the rich
bread whitens into perfect light.

Night of the Fish

Somewhere beneath the earth
blind fish swim colorless in caverns
where light is imagined movement,
an imperceptible lean in an uncompassed direction,
something they feel beneath their scales,
inexplicable and assumed as the waters
of this river that knows no source, no exit.

We travel in the dark air of belief,
in the geometry we desire for death.
Let us be quartz and gold and fool's gold.
Let us be malleable as words
the wind pockets, as foolish as swans.

Would we return to this darkness,
to the stars burning like acid?
Lean back, arms akimbo.
Is your hair a raft of weeds?
Would we wake up again,
just before dawn, the sun beating
like a heart beneath the ribbed horizon?

The Most Terrible and Beautiful Thing

The earth opening, bodies startled
from their graves, lungs like butterflies.
Hearts like matches striking

catch, take hold, not all
at once, but each in its own dark time.
"Is this the moment we were promised?"

They touch each other like the blind.
The past is future, the future closed
forever in the past. Each thing returns

to its beginning, crops to the fields, pasture
to woods, rivers clear to pure thin tongues.
Machines are put to sleep like toothless dogs.

The assassin sips his breakfast coffee
robbed of purpose. Rain climbs
the morning sky. At first, a blessing,

the dead in the arms of their loved ones.
And yet, these poor souls, how mystified
and fierce to see their lives erased,

to know the certain term of infancy,
the seed unspent as fathers steal them
from their earthly home.

How bitter is that death called birth
as our brief time begins, is spent,
and God will not relent.

II

Conversation

"A bird is hiding in your head.
It is opening its wings to soar."

"Yes, but like a hanged man."

The Song the Stone Child Sings

In her womb I turned,
and stroked, and sucked
my dinner down.
I never woke
to a world I did not know.
Face half-finished,
head bent, eyes closed:
which god did I kneel to?

I think it is the god
of silence, the god
of eternal darkness.
Unnamed, I named myself.
I am a small stone
in the womb of love
and I will thrive
after all flesh dies.

Wolf

Gnaw of flesh, skin and tendon cleaving,
furred moons wet as newborn pups.
And the howl of limbs, eyes splintering
light, tongue a body of its own making,
licking clean after, nothing left
but the bone of darkness sucked bright.

The Song the Burnt Child Sings

I have no lips, no nose,
my mouth is a howl,
my tongue a choir.
No one can clap my ears.

I can bite.

Must I thank God for my eyes?
They will not close.
The world spills ceaselessly into them.

If I could have hair or ears,
or nose, or eyes that close,
which would I choose?
None of those.

Lord, give me lips to kiss this life.

Question

The children in her veins are awake now
though they slept awhile ago. They turn
slowly, as one does while waking, and press
their small, blue faces against her skin.
What can they see through this yeasty screen?
The earth of trees, rock, sky? We can see
the slow pulse of their mouths, the exhalation
of dreams. Will they come out, will they
trust air? Or will they nod to sleep again
curled up in the blood's dark lair?

The Song the Suicide Sings

Let the trees still spend their elaborate gestures,
   the air give evidence.
It is good to be home for the last time.
All the comforts of comfort.
The hum, the thousand parts,
a marvel of production, assembly.
Dear ones, my heartland, my oath,
the crime of my crime.
I float, a flower on water.
I hunger for its hunger,
the sweet digestion, the dark
dependency of want. I smell
my death. A miraculous silence.
I can hear the stars breaking.

Mendelssohn at Midnight

Unmerciful music.

The brassy stars are immune.

It is flesh that burns in the pure dark.

The Father's Song

Make me a father, the child says.

The city is a fallen leaf
and I am father of the city,
father of the broken window,
father of distance, father of blight.

Child, spooned into your skin,
give me the faint nape hair
that bends to my breath, give me
the small beginnings of words,

the vowels opening like hands;
give me your hands, your fingers
empty of rings, give me back
language, give me back sorrow.

Words lie down in the grass
like beautiful insects
in their own alien world,
like women in their giving.

And I am father of light, father
of lucid meadows, father of
returnings. I am father
of the blue-veined cock,
father of seed, father of dying.

Games

At dusk the children enter
the tall grass of evening.
They play games with their bodies.
They are looking for something
that is not there, not in the shadows
of their eyes. If I were to ask them
Whose children are you, they would
touch my face with their open mouths
and eat the flesh of my black tears.

The Mother's Last Song

Child, you do not sing
the toad's song
in the iris weeds.

You do not capture fire
in your mouth. You do not
unwind your slithery arms.

In the night of the long grass,
in the night of the black sky,
no flurry of stars.

You are the memory
of your beginning,
another ice age.

In you we find our perfect grave,
the soul pure and rising,
the sea caught in clerical stillness.

She Dreams a Letter from Her Son

Mother, don't hide your dreams in my head.
Mother, my eyes haven't opened yet.
Mother, the days are puppies put to sleep.

Mother, the cottonwoods are crying in the night.
Mother, I am too young to go to school.
Mother, you touched my face and lost your fingers there.

Mother, a gun is a good teacher.
Mother, I have learned my lesson.
Mother, I am staying after school.

The Song the Old Woman Sings

These children are not mine.
When the woman selling tamales comes by
I say to her, *I am a spinster.*
But my belly tells on me.
An ancient face that knows too much,
it stares at me until I turn away.

Why must babies suck beauty from one's breasts?
Fat little ticks, they won't let go
until one's body has closed all its shops
of candles and incense and sweet-smelling soaps.

Yesterday I caught the wrong bus home.
Late, I ran alongside, shouting, beating the door.
The driver let me in. But it was a bus
of children on their way to a museum,
and I sat by their teacher, bewildered
for a moment, afraid
all those faces had found me out.

The Air We Now Breathe

This air is part of the blood
of those who are now dead.
It rises from the grass like sunlight.
Now it enters the lungs of those who survive,
of the children, of the haltered soldiers
where particles of death are filtered to fall
helplessly to the earth, like bodies,
like seeds that will not take root.

The Song the Minister Sings

I am like a woman with two loves.
I would not lie to God.
Will I say the right name?

The old men in libraries read the news for warmth.
When will their names rise up and not their bodies?

Yesterday I prayed for a young man
shrunk to the size of his bones:

Pain, your apron is full.
Thrust that bitter fruit
down his throat. Choke him.

It is the same each day.
I see the children in busses
making tongues and crossed eyes
against the world, laughing at God.

Winter Day

Up here, where our hearts thrive
and our bones burn like logs
it is warm. But our feet know
the coldness of death, the invisible
slain fallen in the snow.
There have been many lost.
We cannot see the bodies
as we step carefully among them.

The Song the Lost Children Sing

The sun is breaking bottles in our eyes.

We are those whose names you do not know
who lift your blood through our hearts.

Are you afraid?

On the shore we sift through your fingers
trying to get back to first things.

We enter the ocean to heal our wounds.
Someone says we are somewhere beyond
the earth's curve, in the whales' cave,
our hands holding nothing but themselves.

We are lanterns lost at sea. There is no help for us.
We are burning into something immortal.
You will discover our names in the houses of fish.

The Way We Are Now

The spirit of bombs
fingers faces on my face.

Sorrow with its stringent ties
generates its own tomorrows.

Ashes sift through the trees,
a fine dust like moonlight.

The Song the Assassin Sings

The knife is a prayer
the flesh answers.

Kneel, an old woman
planting tulips.
I come to bless you.

The isolation
is so beautiful.

To live outside,
to be an alien
in this skin,

to be perfect
beyond your belief.

If there were some other
god I would know him.

Rain After Midnight

The new widow is walking

barefoot on wooden floors

through the early morning hours.

Gnomes

i
The cadence of soldiers,
close all doors

the white sheets fold
their wings in the cupboard

her heart in its nest
a hand of feathers

the scissors set sail
for the shore of her hair

the eyes of the shoe
watch the snake unravel

ii
Lover in your arms,
lie down naked

the mouth is a question
the tongue an answer

ear to the belly,
listen!

a fire in the chimney
the child in its bed

one eye closes
another eye opens

star of the morning
where is the night

Bedtime Story

The fledgling earth
awoke one morning.
The egg had cracked
and the sun settled
her skirts about him
to keep him warm.
The sky blinked
and the earth peeped
in a most endearing
fashion. The sun
nurtured him
until he grew fat
and toddled, a tagalong,
behind her. And she
said, You are a bright boy
and when you grow up
I hope your own children
will be as lovely as you.
And she warmed his feathers
with the flame of her hand.
As the story goes,
he grew, a handsome fellow,
and fathered many children,
mostly beautiful, and some
lived, and some died,
and some broke his heart . . .
"Is there no end to this story?"

My Father's Fortune

Silence was my father's fortune,
carried with him everywhere for safekeeping,
houses and cars and offices crowded with silence.
And trailing my father

four fair-skinned children of different sizes,
a matched set of luggage,
silence folded inside like Sunday clothes.
Everything my father owned transporting silence.

But not a silence of anger or isolation.
Instead, one of yearning, inarticulate
and fumbling. A silence that learned
its own language, its own stubborn love.

Mother at the Mirror, 1939

She says
her lean evening
prayers
for the flesh
fingers dipped
in Pond's
cold cream
blessing
her face
before the bird's-eye
maple dresser
children tucked
asleep
beneath the rim
of wind-whipped
sheets.

Oklahoma Pastoral

The woman snapping beans
from the oak rocker on the east porch
is the one I would marry,
but I am only four, sitting at her feet,
a fly swatter across my lap.

Now I see her rise.
Her chair begins to sing
its own diminished song,
her skirts drift by, winging my face.

I climb from the floor, follow,
swinging the fly swatter, back and forth,
innocent in the buzzing air.

My Father's Bulldogs

i
My father bred bulldogs on Pickard Street.
Our neighbors learned to hate us.
As many as a dozen animals growling and barking.
Misshapen dwarf-dogs, tongues askew,
flies boiling from excrement.

And vicious locked battles in the street.
My father at work.
My mother and my older sisters prying jaws apart
with brooms and mop handles.

Later, exhausted brutes wheezing and moaning.
Crodie, the family pet,
on the back porch, vomiting
behind the wicker clothes hamper.

ii
One night someone slipped into our garage
to tap in the heads of a new litter with a hammer.
Like a cook cracks eggs.

You always think you know who does something like that.
The unemployed brothers who lived across the street
and down with their mother, next door to the house
of the young girl bitten by a black widow spider.

iii
My father brushed the bulldogs' coats for hours,
his quiet Saturday ritual,
trimmed their thick toenails,
taped their ears into roses.

As if *any* human labor could make them beautiful.
I loved Albert Payson Terhune whose dogs were sleek
and lovely, collies with finely tuned heads
who moved like thoroughbred horses. Or dogs
who were half-wild, fathered by wolves,
who became civilized for the love of a human.

iv
My younger sister, Addie, buried Crodie (alive) in her sandbox,
trimmed his ears with blunt-nosed paper scissors.
(Crodie wincing ever-so-slightly, apologetically.)

It was my fault Crodie killed our Easter chickens.
I left their shoebox in the back yard.
My sisters, forgiving, let me attend the funeral.

v
In my room, perched on the edge of the bed,
my mother and father, embarrassed, in straight chairs,
doors closed on older sisters, I failed
What Every Young Boy Should Know.

So my father, shy in sexual matters,
took me to the garage
to watch him breed the bulldogs.

Those hushed evenings, my father's arms
around the bitch holding her steady
as Crodie circled, coughing, sniffing,
until his cock hung slick and limber.

My father, finally, taking the pendulous cock in his hand
to work it in before the fist-sized knot could form.
Crodie's soft black jowls leaking a satisfied drool.

vi

Driving to dog shows late at night with my father
through Oklahoma, Kansas, Missouri, the wing
windows of the Pontiac cranked open,
a stream of air across our faces,
ice-cold Coca-Colas from late-night diners
or vending boxes at filling stations.

Riding in silence through the dark passage of country,
smelling the languid, unclothed land, pungent,
like the body at night, opening, the held heat rising.

Marshmallows

One week I gave Curtiss Saf-T-Pops to every girl
on Pickard Street for kisses, and Mary Lynn,
who loved me best, slapped my face
for no good reason. That week, Maurice broke
his arm falling from the peach tree
onto a pile of flagstones that would never be our patio.
On Saturday we three piled twigs and small branches,
roasted wieners until they curled and split
on the crusted grill. I whittled
poplar branches for marshmallows. Mary Lynn's
were brown and tender as swollen thumbs.
Mine blazed into blackened crusts.
Maurice grew himself a charcoal mustache.
Errol Flynn, wounded hero, home from the war.
"Oh, that? It's nothing. Only a scratch."
Mary Lynn laughed and her green eyes flared
brighter than fireflies. We lay down
on the navy blanket my father sent home
from the Canal Zone and listened to voices
from neighboring houses, the occasional chatter of cars.
Mary Lynn had to go home but Maurice stayed.
I think she loved us both that night.
We heard her singing down the alley,
the creak and slam of her screen door,
and felt too strange to speak.

Evening Dawn

for Sue

I remember an evening on the farm,
my sister and I on the lawn after rain,
young foxes in a green pasture,
the sun gone behind miles of clouds
and the western sky black;

yet a strange green light over all,
crickets sounding in the trees,
leaves like tongues spilling wetness,
the damp breath of their singing;

and my sister and I on the lawn
listening to quail calling,
the evening holding light like the sea,
the sun lost in the deeps of the sky;

yet as if by miracle
a light coming from the east,
from a clear sky beyond massed clouds:
an evening dawn, sending shadows westward;

and we stood in that luminous gift,
in that moment out of order
as if the earth had turned a new orbit,
our lives long shadows before us.

Hearts

"I prefer the dark meat," Mother says,
"so much more flavorful."

"Moist, delicious," Grandmother says.

Father and Grandfather love breast and wishbone.

"Brother loves the heart,"
these women croon, my sisters, too.

Chicken heart, goose heart, duck heart, turkey heart.

"Come to the kitchen, Brother,
your heart is ready!"

Oh, steamy heart gleaming on a white plate.
Jewel, crown, mouthful of joy—
how they sing its praises!

And I, most favored of boys,
come to that warm, stirred room
and chew the heart down.

Farm Dogs

On the farm there were always dogs,
mostly mongrels, shabby brindle,
spotted, or off-white, abandoned
by townspeople, finding their way
up the lane to our house, finding
their way into my heart
through unswerving devotions, companions
of the fields, loafers in the kafir corn
or oats while I mended fence
or worked the posthole digger,
dogs thankful for scraps from supper,
eaters of rabbits, mice from the corn crib,
incessant bearers of pups wedged like potatoes
in the far recesses of the cellar, dogs grateful
not to be kicked or beaten, to be tolerated,
never having slept under a roof,
curled at the foot of a bed, grateful
not to be shot for sport by hunters
or irate farmers, dogs who looked you in the eye,
tongues heavy with happiness.

That Summer

That summer nothing would do
but we sink the boat
in the heart of the lake
and swim in the cool night
for the yellow fire on the beach.

Through the dark water.

We all made it but Ronald,
whom we never found,
who was never Ronald
again; each fish I catch
since, I ask *Ron, is that you?*

The Death and Resurrection of Jesse James

d. April 3, 1882, St. Joseph, Missouri

Oh, the dirty little coward
Who shot Mr. Howard
And laid poor Jesse in his grave

God Bless Our Home
the framed sign
you were straightening
when Bob Ford shot you.
What pitiful desire
I imagine, Zerelda
tapping the nail
into the plaster wall,
near where the bullet
would later flatten,
on Christmas Eve, in 1881,
moving into this strange house
with two small children
and you, Mr. Howard,
a cattle buyer down
on his luck.
You were nearly broke.

Why do I come here
and pay my dollar?
To see brother Frank's
rattlesnake necktie
and stickpin, the pictures
of little Mary and Jesse Edward?
I don't know. Sometimes
the past is more poignant

than we suppose. You were
cruel and crazy, at best.
Yet your tough old mother
sacrificed one leg
to a Pinkerton bomb
thrown through her window
for you, and survived
three husbands and one son.

Jesse, they made your flesh new
sixty and seventy years later,
old, grizzled men wetting
their lips in nursing homes
across the western states
claiming your name, your birth,
but not your death
in that small room.
The escape . . . yes!
The miraculous escape
and the honest life
lived in the shadow
of your legend.
Until, come to this,
it was time to confess,
to embrace whatever honor
the world bestows upon
its dead and risen angels.

I grew up in Oklahoma,
loving your name
and the bearded faces
on the front pages

of slow news days
of the Norman *Transcript*
and the Guthrie *Daily Leader*
wanting them to be
true resurrections.
Wouldn't that be lovely,
if our lives could be reclaimed?
At the auction
after your death
your daughter's high chair
sold for seventy-five cents.
The family dog, the star
of this occasion, was good
for fifteen dollars.
And you? A hero
worthy only of burial space
and intermittent memories
for the brief duration
of two small hearts.

Evening, Milking

Each day redeemed by evening.

The stammering sunset.
The moon in its rut of sky.

The mind is white wicker.

Cows, heavy with the business of milk,
nod home from the east pasture.

There is a moan that milk makes.

The clatter of hooves, the lovely cow eyes.
Thrown oats. The rasp of rough tongues.

My grandmother's small hands.

It is true the earth cries out at dusk.
Its various voices.

To Death, For My Father

Death, this man
is dancing. See
how you can't see
his moves, so quick
his feints confuse,
counter your low
illicit hay-maker
harvesting air, nothing,
which makes you
appear foolish
as he bends double
with sputtering laughter,
and you swing
again, over his head,
losing balance, falling,
surprised at his face
twisted above you, counting.

St. Petersburg, My Father Walks the Beach

Each slow
foot

a lever
lifted

an empty
cylinder

clicked

Poem

The voices of the dead,
how they come back to us,
like apples in summer . . .

Rocking on the east porch
in the shade of chinese elm,
black walnut, iced tea and hot
apple pie, red-skin cheese,
flies itching on the screen . . .

My grandmother's voice
rising above the piano
in the parlor,
Dearie, my dearie, long summer days
have drifted away . . .

The voices of the dead,
they surface
like the heads of swans . . .

IV

Snowstorm on Mozart's Birthday

Kalamazoo, Michigan

The teachers of winter
let down their long hair.

We lie back on our beds
and disappear
in the pale, quiet muslin.

Twenty-seven inches of snow,
and Mozart on the radio.

The neighbors are pushing
through five-foot swells of snow.
Where will they go?

The city is adrift,
but Mozart on the radio.

Mozart, we are thankful.
The air glistens with music
and we lie back again and again.

The sky flings down its lovely notes.
Mozart on the radio.

The Blue Turtle

We cup our hands
against distance, build

a lean-to of knuckles,
kindle a small flame

in the palm of space.
What we own, what we carry.

It is only in the blood-beating
tick of our hearts

against the almost human
whistle of winter

the small blue turtle
each day makes up

a new world, disordered
and reckless, of surprises.

In the Palm of Space

The wishing heart of you I loved, Kalamazoo
—Carl Sandburg

i

Infinite is the string
that pulls the darkness out,
turns a pocket into daylight,

an ear of moon
listening to the earth
above the long horizon.

The houses of the city
flush with desire,
each window a sunrise.

ii

Someone is waking, her face
at the window, a woman
in a pink slip beckoning.

Will it avail us not to go?

Will we remember
her familiar gestures,
her words already spoken?

She leans one hand
on the bird's-eye dresser,
hip slung in the warm glint

of her slip, her body
the sleeve we touch,
longingly, in a crowd.

iii
When evening comes
and the air is blue and kindly,
she rubs her hands for warmth,
the small fire spitting
from crumpled paper and kindling
sparks like hyphens.

Distance is always there,
in the crevices of speech,
in the cramped quarters
of the moon. She thinks the moon
is a mouth, a smile or a cry
we disregard, trying to keep
the blood in. We don't want
out, we want in. The chains
around our shoulders, the hulls
of sleep, her head nestled in the pit
of his arm circling her body,
the rope she dangles from.

Climb out or climb in,
don't fall, a stone
down mountain slopes,
your neck bending, graceful
as a wrist, hesitant
clouds of breath like dust
rising and settling, your face,
the head thrown back, suddenness
of desire, toppled, the bite of earth.

iv
A man is walking his dog,
the snow falling in thick clusters,
small, fat fists of snow. The dog
shakes her coat, a flurry

of fleas dislodged, a game
of blind man's bluff.
The bandage removed,
the eyes have disappeared.

How strange to be alone,
someone's children crying
from their beds,

little large-eyed owls.
A dumb show
of trees against the sky.

Wood explodes as it dies,
the ring of years released
in flame and smoke,
as when the mind goes.

Our bodies in drifts,
tinder for the fire.

Ten degrees, wet muzzles
paint the windows. Inside,
a woman sleeps, her hand pale and open
like an empty eye socket.

v

She has been closed, now,
for some months,
like a room after a death.
The bed has been made
with clean sheets.
But no one sleeps there.

In the garden she sees
her face in the cabbage

still growing from the earth,
its thick white root. She twists
with two hands cupped
over the ears, no Mozart,
no Schubert, snaps the head loose,
carries it on her hip, in the crook
of her arm, like a child
needing to be spanked. She sets it
on the kitchen table, her mother's
table, oak and scars, old wax
and varnish, where it rocks
in its chair and is no longer her face.

The worms come,
an onslaught of commas,
disconnected phrases, leaves
falling like words, not praising
the air or the earth, finding fault,
the tree caught in a web
of its own making,
worms smirking in the drift
of their silken parachutes,
ribbed leaves shot through,
ventricles of air sobbing,
the worms hanging
like sacks of hearts
sucking up all the blood,
embryos curbed and feeding.
Her tree, its fruit hard green polyps
strewn, splitting, blackening.

vi

The corpse of a barn lies
in a heap on the black soil.
You see others in Michigan,
Oklahoma, perhaps anywhere

in this country, gone too far,
a terminal illness. The old lady
dead, what's the use? Who's to plant
flowers, paint the mailbox?
So it's left to rot,
a slow corpse, perhaps
twenty years to collapse
into the earth. Is the smell
in the wood, the rot,
the angle of boards?

vii

Lie with me, old woman,
in the river's murky bed,
in the fellowship of water.

The morning fog,
eddies of morning fog.

Black-and-white cows
standing in the stilled water,
drinking deeply, tails singing,
the old motion, the same story.
Two on the river bank under
a tree, six in the water, udder deep.

Let me kneel in the thick mud,
take the swarthy, warted teats
in my hands. The mooing river.

viii

The woman with two husbands hangs
sheets on the line. Will they dry
in time? Her hands are sparrows
on her thighs. She prepares:
How will it be? She sweetens

her body. One man turns the corner
of her mouth. She tastes him.
She practices the other's name.
One loves her fallen breasts,
the long nipples naming
the earth, the way she falls back
into the caves of the bed, her body
parting like a loaf of bread.

One palms the sun,
slips it into his pocket.
He's keeping it for her hair.

ix
She doesn't want to lie down
among strangers, their buttocks
stiffening into shell,
two skulls beneath her palms.
They lower above her
like the sun coming down,
for a moment the reddest sky
she has ever seen.

In this cascade of noons
and loosened ties, of afternoons
spilled from the torn pockets
of travellers, of disembodied words,
motes in air shafts, sunlight drifting
pellucid snow, this is you
knowing your life is more
than you can ever earn, this
is you in the distant shadows
watching yourself so tangible
in sleep, as if you could
reach out and touch your life.

x

Beneath the ice, in February,
something frozen awaits
the hiss of yesses, spins
in the cold bark of wings.
Leaves sigh like children asleep,
the earth questions winter.

A man and a woman are walking
in a marsh. She touches him.
His skin clings to her fingers
everywhere she turns.

xi

Is there a death we experience after death?
The eyes of rocks glinting through centuries.

The tumble of stars.

We lie back in the sweet grass,
spent and out of breath.

Our mouthless speech is such
we imagine the dead would know.

We sleep. Among all those voices.

xii

Someone is mowing after dark.

The path is a fresh, damp
green, the mad cylinder

whirling, shooting up
little sparks of grass.
It must hurt those trees

to be so green. The sky
riffling its feathers, the earth
a nest of twigs and string,
a few bottle caps. If we could understand
the day's dear gibberish
we would ring its tin cup with coin.

xiii

The sunlight must be said,
the way it sings
as it strolls across the city,
hands in its pockets.
And the clean laundry of clouds.
We must say how we slip
into these clothes
as if our bodies were
transparent as vowels.

Her yeasty breasts wet and warm,
and he comes, lovely fish,
mysterious breather, climbing
from the ocean, taking hold
of air, lungs unfurling. She
catches him in her two hands,
wet weather, gull cry, turtle crawl.

Painted Lady. Pearly
Eye. Mourning Cloak.
The sun has learned
to touch the wings open.
They swell, divide like lips.
Salves of birth smooth their entry,
the giving way and the giving.
This world where flight is possible.

xiv
The girl lugging her satchel of surprises
to school may give them up,
one by one, until
she is empty of desire.
Today, a blackbird would flip
out, unzipped, a word
sleeping on its tongue,
the word we hunger for.

Our children may rise to new life
if we give birth, breath, name,
to that which yet may live.

xv
Call the children in,
supper on the table.
Dusk, a skitter of starlings
in the ravine, skateboards
on the pavement.
A woman rakes leaves
along the width of her yard,
her small hands placed
so and so on the long handle
of the rake, a sinewy strength
in her arms, in the fury
of her labor, the wheel of leaves
flung into the air, spinning,
climbing, a froth of leaves
like water set into motion
by the tide of her body,
everything caught up
in the undertow,
twigs, stones,
dirt, until
the woman—laughing, crying—

leaps deeply into that surf,
drowning, rising up.

xvi
We will be late in traffic.

Glasses shed frost
on the marble counter.

Above the mirror
time tells its usual story.

And then in the moon
of the wakened flesh
we listen to the lisp
of our bodies, delicate
as light the tongue sheds,
delicate as the crevices of mica,
as her voice saying
there, there, there,
and the nose is an animal
burrowing, a snail
shell, a house at dusk
where a woman without thinking
wipes her palms on
the curve of her hips,
spoons heaped with dessert.

Small fragments of rescue.

The hand, no matter
how crippled, how betrayed
saved by the warmth
of blessed skin and flesh.
No comfort like this,
burning and burning, tender
and tentative recognitions.

xvii
Kalamazoo, you are wealthy
with spring. The shelves
of your trees are stocked
with green. I can hear the hidden
discourse. The momentary
whirlpools of leaves.
The grass is deep, unmowed.
Too late.
The dandelions have scattered
their million seeds.

The fur that pearls the underside
of leaves, the down on upper
lip, the purse of cheek bone,
lobe of ear, the way a blossom
furls, unfurls. Sweet intercourse,
the moisture's tongue
taking its curl of honey,
the rub and welt of taste.

xviii
Is this the day we save ourselves?

The earth welcomes us
into the shuddering dark.

Let the dirt clean and shine
our hearts, let us peel
to the pure cave of the soul.

Mother night, shake out the stars.

Poem

for Shirley

Isn't it here
in the unnamed
giving of light,
bodies of earth and water
lifted and taken
into the orbit of flesh;
isn't it the waking
of blood and bone
to another earthly presence
moving across the space
of a lighted window
as though it were
the universe;
isn't it the breaking
that sets free
the commingling of sane
and insane fragments
moments when the light
burns through
to the meek
suspension of air?